Serengeti Journey
On Safari in Africa

By Gare Thompson

NATIONAL GEOGRAPHIC

Washington D.C.

One of the world's largest nonprofit scientific and educational organizations, the National Geographic Society was founded in 1888 "for the increase and diffusion of geographic knowledge." Fulfilling this mission, the Society educates and inspires millions every day through its magazines, books, television programs, videos, maps and atlases, research grants, the National Geographic Bee, teacher workshops, and innovative classroom materials. The Society is supported through membership dues, charitable gifts, and income from the sale of its educational products. This support is vital to National Geographic's mission to increase global understanding and promote conservation of our planet through exploration, research, and education.

For more information, please call
1-800-NGS-LINE (647-5463) or write to the following address:
National Geographic Society
1145 17th Street N.W.
Washington, D.C. 20036-4688
U.S.A.

For information about special discounts for bulk purchases, please contact
National Geographic Books Special Sales at ngspecsales@ngs.org

Visit the Society's Web site: www.nationalgeographic.com

Copyright © 2006 National Geographic Society

Text revised from *On Safari* in the National Geographic Windows on Literacy program from National Geographic School Publishing, © 2002 National Geographic Society

All rights reserved. Reproduction of the whole or any part of the contents without written permission from the publisher is prohibited.

Published by National Geographic Society. Washington, D.C. 20036

Design by Project Design Company

Printed in the United States

**Library of Congress
Cataloging-in-Publication Data**

Thompson, Gare.
Serengeti journey : on safari in Africa / by Gare Thompson.
    p. cm. -- (National Geographic science chapters)
Includes bibliographical references and index.
ISBN-13: 978-0-7922-5952-7 (library binding)
ISBN-10: 0-7922-5952-1 (library binding)
1. Mammals--Tanzania--Serengeti Plain. 2. Safaris--Tanzania--Serengeti Plain. I. Title. II. Series.
QL731.T35T46 2006
599.09678'27--dc22

                              2006016335

Photo Credits
Front Cover: © PhotoDisc/ Getty Images; Spine: © Timothy G. Laman/ National Geographic Image Collection; Endpaper: © Stuart Westmorland/ Getty Images; 0-1: © Ferrero-Labat/ Auscape; 4: © Medford Taylor/National Geographic Image Collection; 5: © Frank Krahmer/ zefa/ Corbis; 6-7: © Timothy G. Laman/ National Geographic Image Collection; 8-9: © PhotoDisc/ Getty Images; 9: © Jason Edwards/ Bio-images; 10: © M&C Denis Huot-Bios/ Auscape; 12: © Joel Sartore/ National Geographic Image Collection; 13, 14: © Ferrero-Labat/ Auscape; 15: © ANT Photo Library; 16, 17 (left): © Ferrero-Labat/ Auscape; 17 (right): © Jason Edwards/ Bio-images; 18, 20-21: © ANT Photolibrary; 23 (all): © Fritz Polking/ Auscape; 24, 25: © Ferrero-Labat/ Auscape; 26: © Beverly Joubert/ National Geographic Image Collection; 28-29: © Renee Lynn/ Stone/ Getty Images; 30-31: © Ferrero-Labat/ Auscape; 31 (top): © Michael Nichols/ National Geographic Image Collection; 32: © Ferrero-Labat/ Auscape; 33: © ANT Photo Library; 34 (top): © Ferrero-Labat/ Auscape; 34 (bottom): © Beverly Joubert/ National Geographic Image Collection; 35: © Chris Johns/ National Geographic Image Collection; Map by National Geographic Maps.

Contents

A giraffe walks across the Serengeti Plain.

The Serengeti

Let's go on a safari. The word safari comes from an Arabic word that means "journey." A hundred years ago, people went on a safari in Africa to hunt wild animals. Today, people go on a safari to observe wild animals and take pictures of them. On a safari you can see how animals live in the wild.

▶ Crested cranes live on the grasslands of the Serengeti.

Land and Climate

We are going to the Serengeti Plain in East Africa. The name Serengeti means "endless plains." The Serengeti are the grasslands of Africa. Here you will see tall grasses and a few trees. You'll see small rivers, lakes, and even swamps.

Acacia trees grow among the grasses on the Serengeti Plain.

On the Serengeti, it is warm year round. There are two main seasons—a dry season and a rainy season. From June through October, the Serengeti is dry. The rainy season begins in November, with the heaviest of the rains falling between March and May.

The Animals of the Serengeti

Millions of large animals roam these grasslands. Many of them live in national parks. The government sets up these parks to protect Africa's rich wildlife. Here you will see many different animals. There are lions, cheetahs, zebras, and elephants. There are giraffes, monkeys, and lots of water animals. The Serengeti is the perfect place to study animals.

Many scientists come here to study animals. They watch how the animals act. They see what the animals eat. They track the animals to see where they go. They see how the animals take care of their young.

On our safari, we'll study three very different animals. Stay together. Take careful notes. Draw pictures if you want to. Try not to scare the animals.

AFRICA

SERENGETI
PLAIN

▲ Tourists come to
see the large
animals that roam
the grasslands.

Chapter 1

Giraffes

The giraffe is the tallest of all land animals. Its long neck is what makes it so tall. The giraffe has seven bones in its neck. That's the same number of neck bones that you have, but the giraffe's bones are huge! Most male giraffes stand about 19 feet (6 meters) tall. Females are a little shorter.

Giraffes have dark brown spots. The spots form a pattern on their yellow fur. The spots are pretty to look at, but they also help protect giraffes. When giraffes are feeding on the trees, their spots help to hide them.

Being so tall helps giraffes survey the landscape.

A giraffe's horns are covered with fur.

Notice the giraffe's large head. The first thing you probably see are its horns. Some giraffes have two horns, but others have four.

Can you find its nostrils? They are the two slits at the end of its nose. A giraffe's nostrils can open and close. Winds blow sand and dirt around. The giraffe closes its nostrils to keep out sand and dirt.

Sight is the giraffe's most important sense. Look at its large eyes high on its head. It is the first animal on the Serengeti to spot an enemy. When a giraffe sees an enemy, it runs away. Giraffes have long legs. They can run fast. Sometimes, they use their hard hooves to kick an enemy. But giraffes are peaceful animals. They do not have many enemies.

Giraffes can run as fast as 35 miles (56 km) an hour for short distances.

Eating in the Wild

Watch a giraffe eat. It stretches its long neck to the top of a tree. There it finds fresh green leaves. Most animals cannot reach food this high. We see some giraffes eating from an acacia tree. Acacia leaves are their favorite food. But some giraffes also eat twigs and thorns. Eating from trees like this is called browsing.

▲ A giraffe uses its tongue to pull leaves off trees.

Giraffes have very long tongues. A giraffe's tongue can be over a foot and a half (46 centimeters) long. Giraffes curl their long tongues around the leaves and tear them off. A giraffe eats like a cow or sheep. It chews its cud. That means that it chews food twice before digesting it.

Giraffes can go a long time without drinking water. But when they do drink, they have to be careful. Giraffes usually go to a watering hole together so they can take turns watching for predators. Look at the way the giraffe on the left is bent over to drink. Think how easily a lion could attack it.

▼ A giraffe must spread its legs far apart to ·be able to reach the water.

A female giraffe watches over two calfs.

Giraffe Families

Giraffes live together in small groups. The young giraffes play together. Several of the female giraffes, called aunts, watch all the young. The aunts take care of the young while the other giraffes feed. They clean them and help them get food. They also protect the young from predators.

Female giraffes can have babies when they are five years old. The baby, or calf, is born after 15 months. At birth, the calf is about 6 feet (2 meters) tall. The mother stands when giving birth. This means that the calf drops to the ground when it is born. But it is not hurt. Within 30 minutes, the calf can stand on its long, wobbly legs.

How do giraffes sleep? They can sleep standing up or lying down. But giraffes do not sleep for long periods of time. Most sleep for only three or four minutes at a time. They doze more than sleep.

▲ Two giraffes look for food at dawn.

◄ Two giraffes play together.

Chapter 2

Cheetahs

The cheetah looks like a big cat. It weighs from 80 to 140 pounds (34–74 kilograms). The cheetah is large, but fast. It is the fastest land animal. The cheetah can run over 60 miles (97 kilometers) per hour. That is as fast as cars go!

The cheetah has a body that helps it run fast. It has long, thin legs that are very powerful. Its legs give it great speed.

The cheetah has a small head and a flat face. It has large eyes and excellent eyesight. It can see long distances.

Cheetahs live on the grasslands of the Serengeti.

See the cheetah's tan coat. It has black spots on it. With its spotted coat, the cheetah is hard to see in the tall grass. The cheetah also has spots on its tail. Look at the end of its tail. It looks like a paintbrush.

A cheetah can run very fast for short distances.

The cheetah has short claws that help it grip the ground as it runs. The pads of its feet are hard like tire treads. This helps the cheetah make sharp turns. Few animals can escape a cheetah.

Eating in the Wild

Unlike the giraffe, the cheetah eats meat. It hunts its prey. The cheetah is a good hunter. Let's observe the cheetah hunting.

First, the cheetah uses its eyes to spot its prey. Most cheetahs hunt during the day when it is easy to see. They hunt in the early morning or the late afternoon.

The cheetah follows, or stalks, its prey from a distance. It often follows herds of antelopes or gazelles.

Then, the cheetah gives chase. It quickly brings down its prey. Its powerful jaws grip the gazelle. The animal cannot breathe and dies. The cheetah has found its meal.

The cheetah rests before it eats. Other animals sometimes try to steal the cheetah's food while it is resting. But these animals have to move fast or hope that the cheetah has fallen asleep. Animals know that they cannot outrun the cheetah.

A cheetah gives chase and brings down an antelope.

Cheetah Families

Many cheetahs live alone. Others live in small groups. Listen to them. They do not roar like other large cats. They whine or growl. A cub makes a chirping sound to call its mother.

The female gives birth after carrying her babies for three months. She has a litter of four to six cubs. The cubs are small when they are born. The mother finds a quiet, hidden spot for the cubs. This hidden spot will keep the cubs safe. Cubs are a favorite food for lions.

Tall grass hides the cubs, keeping them safe.

Cheetah cubs practice their hunting skills.

The cubs begin to follow the mother around when they are six weeks old. As they play, they learn to hunt. See the cubs pretending to hunt. Sometimes the cubs chase prey that is too big for them to kill. But they keep trying.

The cubs stay with their mother until they are about 18 months old. Then they leave. Often, the male cubs stay together. They form a group that can last for the rest of their lives.

Chapter 3

Elephants

What is the first thing that you observe about elephants? It probably is their size. Elephants are the biggest land animal in the world. Male elephants weigh about 6 tons (5,500 kilograms)! Do you see how thick their skin is? This helps protect them. They can go through thick thorns without being hurt. What else do you see?

Elephants have tusks. Tusks are teeth that never stop growing. They are long, pointed, and curved. They are made out of ivory. Hunters kill elephants for their tusks.

An elephant eats grasses on the Serengeti Plain.

Look at the elephant's trunk. An adult elephant's trunk is about seven feet (2 meters) long. An elephant uses its trunk for holding things, eating, and drinking. Elephants also use their trunks to pick up dirt and spray themselves. The dirt cools them off and gets rid of bugs, too.

A young elephant uses its trunk to spray dust on its back.

The elephant is large, but its eyes are small. They are about the size of a golf ball. What color are they? Most elephants' eyes are a golden or green color.

Elephants are smart animals. They have the largest brain of all land animals. Let's watch them in the wild.

Eating in the Wild

Remember how big elephants are? Well, they have to eat a lot of food. Most elephants eat about 300 pounds (136 kilograms) of food each day! That is why we see the elephants moving. They are always looking for food.

Elephants eat many things. They eat grass and leaves. They also eat bulbs, berries, and tree bark. Like the giraffe, elephants love to eat acacia trees. Watch them. See how the elephant gathers food with its trunk and puts it in its mouth. Elephants can also use their tusks to strip off bark from trees. They can use their trunks to pick up nuts from the ground.

An elephant uses its trunk to gather food and drink water.

► An elephant uses its tusks to strip bark from a tree.

Elephant Families

Elephants live in family groups called herds. Elephants can live to be 60 to 70 years old. So these herds stay together for a long time.

See those two elephants with their trunks together? They are "kissing." Elephants play and live together. The male elephant is called a bull. The female is called a cow.

Like the giraffe, the elephant gives birth standing up. But the elephant carries its baby almost two years before it is born. The young calf gets milk from its mother until it is about three years old. Then it starts to eat

▼ Elephants show affection by wrapping their trunks together.

▲ **Elephants help a calf cross a stream.**

grass. The calves stay with the herd until they are about 13 years old. Then they often join another herd.

Unlike giraffes or cheetahs, elephants sniff danger. They use their trunk to do this. When an animal comes too near, elephants flap their ears and make a frightening sound. Then they charge at top speed. The elephants work as a group to protect each other.

Elephants may be big, but they are gentle and caring. They live together and look out for each other much the way our own families do.

Chapter 4

What Did You Observe?

Giraffes, elephants, and cheetahs all live on the grasslands of the Serengeti. Think about how these animals live, what they eat, and how they take care of their families. How are these animals alike? How are they different?

How to Write an A+ Report

1. Choose a topic.
- Find something that interests you.
- Make sure it is not too big or too small.

2. Find sources.
- Ask your librarian for help.
- Use many different sources: books, magazine articles, and websites.

3. Gather information.
- Take notes. Write down the big ideas and interesting details.
- Use your own words.

4. Organize information.
- Sort your notes into groups that make sense.

- Make an outline. Put your groups of notes in the order you want to write your report.

5. Write your report.

- Write an introduction that tells what the report is about.

- Use your outline and notes as you write to make sure you say everything you want to say in the order you want to say it.

- Write an ending that tells about your report.

- Write a title.

6. Revise and edit your report.

- Read your report to make sure it makes sense.

- Read it again to check spelling, punctuation, and grammar.

7. Hand in your report!

Glossary

aunt	a female giraffe that cares for young giraffes
browse	to eat by nibbling on leaves
bull	a male elephant
calf	a baby giraffe or elephant
cow	a female elephant
cub	a baby cheetah
cud	food that an animal has not digested and brings up from the stomach to chew again
herd	a group of elephants
national park	an area set aside to protect wildlife
nostril	one of two openings at the end of a nose through which an animal breathes
prey	an animal that is hunted by another animal for food
safari	a trip or journey to hunt or look at wild animals
stalk	to quietly follow or hunt an animal
tusk	one of a pair of long, curved pointed teeth on an elephant

Further Reading

• Books •

Bateman, Robert. *Safari*. Boston, MA: Little, Brown and Company, 1998. Ages 9-12, 32 pages.

Lekuton, Joseph Lemasolai. *Facing the Lion: Growing Up Maasai on the African Savanna*. Washington, DC: National Geographic Society, 2004. Ages 10-14, 144 pages.

Wexo, John Bonnett. *Elephants (Zoobook Series)*. Poway, CA: Wildlife Education, Ltd, 2002. Ages 9-12, 18 pages.

Wexo, John Bonnett. *Giraffes (Zoobook Series)*. Poway, CA: Wildlife Education, Ltd, 2001. Ages 9-12, 18 pages.

Wood, Linda C. *Cheetahs (Zoobook Series)*. Poway, CA: Wildlife Education, Ltd, 2000. Ages 9-12, 18 pages.

• Websites •

Serengeti National Park
http://www.serengeti.org/

Cheetahs:
National Geographic Society
www.nationalgeographic.com/kids/creature_feature/0003/

Public Broadcasting Service
http://www.pbs.org/wnet/nature/cheetahs/

Elephants:
National Geographic Society
www.nationalgeographic.com/kids/creature_feature/0103/

Public Broadcasting Service
http://www.pbs.org/wnet/nature/elephants/

Giraffes:
National Geographic Society
www.nationalgeographic.com/kids/creature_feature/0111/

Kids Planet
http://www.kidsplanet.org/factsheets/giraffe.html

Index